OXFORD
UNIVERSITY PRESS

What Do You Want to Be?

Contents

Introduction

Have you ever thought about what you would like to be when you grow up? Here are some jobs that people do. Which one would you like to do?

Astronaut

Astronauts do many different tasks on a spaceship.

An astronaut is a person who flies into outer space in a spaceship. Astronauts do not spend all their time in outer space. Sometimes, they work at a ground base. At the ground base astronauts learn how to fly, land and fix a spaceship.

This astronaut is floating outside a spaceship.

If you want to be an astronaut you will need to train for many years. You will have to learn how to live in small spaces inside the spaceship.

Would you like to be an astronaut?

Teacher

A teacher teaches her students about using a computer.

Teachers help people learn.

A teacher helps children and adults learn. Some teachers teach in nurseries. Some teachers teach in schools and some teachers teach at universities.

An art teacher and his students are working outside.

If you want to be a teacher you will also need to train for a long time. You will have to like working with people.

Would you like to be a teacher?

Doctor

A doctor is a person who helps people when they are ill. Some doctors help with all illnesses. Other doctors look after one part of the body, like the throat or the heart.

A doctor can see what is wrong when your throat is sore.

Doctors train for a long time, like astronauts and teachers. Some doctors become surgeons. This means they operate on people who are ill.

Would you like to be a doctor?

Fashion Designer

Fashion designers draw their clothes designs.

A fashion designer is a person who designs clothes. Some fashion designers work in large clothing companies. Some fashion designers work by themselves.

Fashion designers learn how to draw their designs. They learn how to make patterns. If you want to be a fashion designer you will need to be able to sew.

Would you like to be a fashion designer?

Models wear designers' clothes to show them off. ▼

Olympic Swimmer

An Olympic swimmer swims to win races and medals. Olympic swimmers train every day. They eat special foods to give them energy to train hard. They have a coach who shows them how to swim faster.

A swimming coach shows a swimmer how to get better at swimming.

Some Olympic swimmers teach children to swim. They try to teach them what they have learned.

Would you like to be an Olympic swimmer?

This swimmer coaches some children.

Dentist

A dentist takes care of people's teeth. Dentists clean people's teeth and fill any holes. Sometimes, they take teeth out. Dentists also teach people how to look after their teeth, so that they will not need fillings.

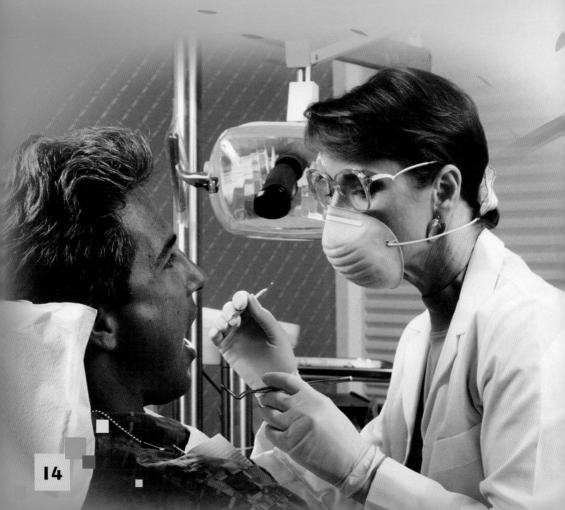

Braces make teeth grow straight.

If you clean your teeth well, it will help keep them healthy.

If you want to be a dentist you will have to train for a long time. You will have to learn how to use special tools like a small drill.

Would you like to be a dentist?

15

Firefighter

Firefighters have to put out fires. They have special clothes to protect them. They wear hard hats to protect their heads. They wear strong boots to protect their feet.

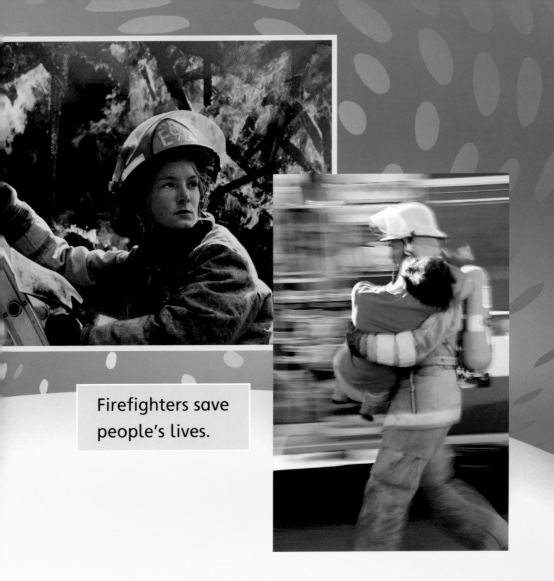

Firefighters save people's lives.

Firefighters go to fires in fire engines. They go very fast. Sometimes, they have to rescue people from burning houses or high buildings.

Would you like to be a firefighter?

Jockey

A jockey is someone who rides horses in races.
Racehorses run very fast. Jockeys have to be
very fit.

Jockeys wear different coloured hats. The tops
that jockeys wear are called 'silks'.

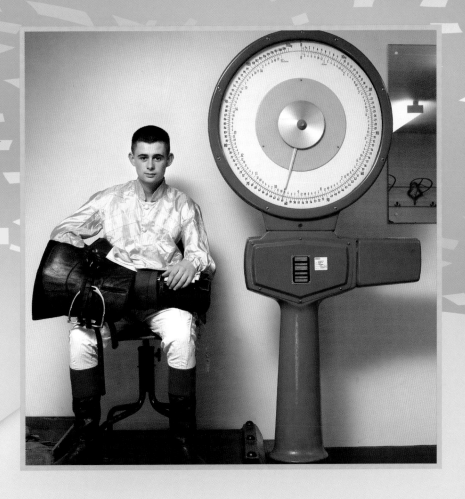

Jockeys have to be small and light so that they do not weigh their horses down. They have to be weighed before each race to make sure they are not too heavy.

Would you like to be a jockey?

Electrician

An electrician is a person who puts the wires and plugs and switches into your house to make the electricity work. The wires have to be connected together in the right way.

Some electricians do not work on houses. They work on the high power lines outside. Some electricians work in power stations.

Would you like to be an electrician?

Police Officer

A police officer helps people stay safe. Sometimes, police officers control the traffic. Sometimes, police officers work with animals. They work with horses and dogs.

This police officer is working with a specially trained dog.

Police officers help in a road accident.

You can ask a police officer to tell you the way if you are lost.

Some police officers wear special clothes. Some police officers drive special cars.

Would you like to be a police officer?

Index